CHANGING TIDES

CHANGING TIDES

A Pact Press Anthology

Edited by Jaynie Royal and Michelle Rosquillo

Pact Press

Published by Pact Press
An imprint of
Regal House Publishing, LLC
Raleigh, NC 27612
All rights reserved

https://pactpress.com

Printed in the United States of America

ISBN -13 (paperback): 9781646031597
Library of Congress Control Number: 2020936511

Interior and cover design by Lafayette & Greene
lafayetteandgreene.com
Cover images © by Rich Carey/Shutterstock

Regal House Publishing, LLC
https://regalhousepublishing.com

A Regal House Initiative Project
a 503(c) entity
-the nonprofit arm of Regal House Publishing-

Printed in the United States of America

THE CORAL RESTORATION FOUNDATION

Net proceeds from the sale of this work benefit the Coral Restoration Foundation™.

Coral Restoration Foundation™ is a 501 3 (c) non-profit organization that was founded in 2007 in response to the widespread loss of the dominant coral species on the Florida Reef Tract. Coral Restoration Foundation™ (CRF) now manages the largest coral restoration program in the world.

Coral Restoration Foundation™ works to support the reefs' natural recovery processes through the large-scale cultivation, outplanting, and monitoring of genetically diverse, reef-building corals. Their mission is to restore coral reefs, to educate others on the importance of our oceans, and to use science to further coral research and coral reef monitoring techniques.

To learn more, and to get involved in the mission to save and restore our planet's coral reefs, visit www.coralrestoration.org

Contents

Foreword

Alice Grainger

As is evident in this profound collection of vignettes, humans have a primal connection with the ocean. The sea, which covers more than seventy percent of our planet, has been a source of inspiration and folklore since time immemorial, synonymous with life's enduring mystery, with freedom, change, and the unknown.

We make pilgrimages to the beach, drawn by the pellucid pull of turquoise waters, the expansive wonder of the waves stretching over the horizon, mesmerized by the promise of the abundant life that teems beneath the surface.

But our connection with the ocean is as physical as it is metaphysical—it is thought that life on Earth began in the sea some four billion years ago, around deep, hydrothermal vents. And even today our lives still begin inside a tiny, saline sea—as embryos we gestate inside our mothers within a safe and salty pool that echoes of the dawn of life on our home world. Once we emerge, the salinity in our veins mirrors the salinity of the sea; we still carry the ocean within us.

Every breath we take connects us with the waters of our planet; seventy percent of the oxygen we breathe is produced by marine plants. The oceans and the life they support are critical for our own survival, and yet we are contributing to their destruction.

For more than 500 million years, coral reefs have inhabited our shallow seas. They are some of the oldest and most biodiverse ecosystems on Earth, supporting at least twenty-five percent of all marine life, forming vital natural barriers that protect coastlines from storms, providing critical protein for billions of people, and underpinning economies around the world. Yet, in the last thirty years, we have lost half of our planet's shallow water coral reefs.

Coral reefs that once captivated visitors with wondrous life and color are quickly becoming graveyards, nightmarish vistas of bleached bones molded over by algae. It is predicted that by the end of this century, all coral reefs could disappear. This would be the first time in human history that we will have witnessed the disappearance of an entire biome and we simply have no idea what the consequences of this would be for all life on Earth.

Coral Restoration Foundation™ is providing a solution, restoring damaged reefs on a massive scale using simple, effective, science-based techniques that we are sharing with the world. Learning from nature, we can support the coral reefs' natural processes of recovery and provide hope for the future of these magnificent, crucial ecosystems. But we can't do this alone, we need the world to get involved.

Painters, writers, and poets have always defined the zeitgeist. Art and literature drive the evolution of our societal consciousness. Songs of the ocean and its inhabitants have been passed down to us through generations, but we are now entering a time where these songs of the sea speak of despair, and of dying. While the dramatic loss and ongoing destruction of marine life is not an easy fact to face, forging an emotional connection with our ocean and the challenges it faces is critical if we are to generate support for its protection.

And so the voices in this anthology are cause for optimism.

Let them speak to you, let their words resonate and inspire you to move forward, motivated to take action.

Every ecosystem is interconnected. All that we need to do to turn the tide is to find one cause that speaks to us, to choose one change and devote ourselves to it. We all have the capacity to make a difference, and the time to make that difference is now.

Alice Grainger
Communications Director, Coral Restoration Foundation™
Key Largo, Florida, February 2020
www.coralrestoration.org

When I Heard There Was an Ocean

Susan Bruce

When I heard there was an ocean
with ragged breaks and undertows

I only thought of myself, a note that plays
over and over. Sometimes I am in good humor.

Often, by nature my heart goes out
and I am finally paying attention.

The ocean decamps to slow bones bending.
I follow. I am sure I make them nervous.

AN OCEAN

Susan Bruce

orchard of
waves drift
past & future.

I swim
in the longing
of here we are
altogether again.

I do my best.
I am useful.
I am living up to.

The wind is
picking up.
It has a duty
to come back
as if the cure.

SEA KEEPER

Susan Bruce

When I first slipped on a wave it ran me over.
A mythic sea keeper pulls me
close to not-wanting and says
It's time. This is where you come in.
Now I think of the sea joining in.

Susan Bruce has a chapbook from Finishing Line Press
(2015) called *Body of Water*, as well as poems published by
Washington Square Press, Barrow Street, *805*, *SWWIM*, *The
Inquisitive Eater*, *Finery*, *Dirty Chai*, YESYES Book, *Yes Poetry*,
No Dear, and *34th Parallel*.

Pretzels and a Problem of Scale

Christina Stefan

Complimentary pretzels make me think about the ocean. Let me rephrase: I think about the ocean a lot when I fly. Scaling consumption is a difficult concept to fathom. We intimately understand only that which we touch—the items we choose to purchase, use, and dispose of. Those numbers aren't so significant. After all, I'm just one person. If I buy a Monday morning coffee in a disposable coffee cup, that only adds up to fifty-two cups a year. That's not so bad, right?

I find it's easier to remember scale when I travel. I'm no longer an individual; I'm one unit in a huge system that moves people around the globe day in and day out. My contemplation of scale begins as the plane lifts off and a city block that once seemed large dwindles into one of thousands. It's hard to imagine the true scale of something when you yourself are so small. It's only when you zoom out that you can readjust your perspective.

Likewise, the ocean is so vast, so incomprehensible. On a clear day, the human eye can see approximately three miles to the horizon. The Pacific Ocean covers more than sixty million square miles—a vastness incomprehensible to the average human. We can only touch it in traces—a beach trip here, a boat ride there. With a scale that massive, it seems untouchable. Mankind's effect on it was out of sight, out of mind for most people until, in 2015, a now infamous video began to circulate of an Olive Ridley sea turtle with a straw lodged in its nose. We were suddenly forced to grapple with

8

this butterfly effect. *Surely it wasn't my straw that made its way into this turtle's nose?* Well, it was someone's. I'm shaken out of my musings by the flight attendant. The seatbelt sign has gone off and he is offering me a complimentary beverage—a luxury afforded by the high price tag for this flight. Along with this, he offers a snack pack demurely displayed on a napkin to catch the crumbs. My one cup, my one napkin, my one tiny bag of complimentary pretzels.

It's only when I once again begin zooming out that I get a sense of the problem. This one cup might be made of a recyclable plastic, but many airlines still aren't recycling, and multiple countries require the incineration of anything that poses a contamination risk. That napkin is certainly waste; materials contaminated by food are destined for a landfill. That bag of pretzels? A non-recyclable layered vessel of propylene, polyethelene, and resin. Even more so than marriage, when two materials are brought together, no recycling plant can tear them asunder.

A 737, one of the most popular airplanes airlines buy, can hold anywhere from 85 to 215 passengers. I see my one bag of pretzels, then see my seatmate's one bag of pretzels, and the person's next to them, then those of the people behind us, and the numbers begin to add up. American Airlines, the airline I fly with the most, shuttles approximately 500,000 people a day. That's a lot of non-recyclable bags of pretzels.

The growth of single-use goods—particularly plastic ones—in our culture is a bizarre one. The advent of plastic was a revolution. Mankind was no longer constrained to natural materials; we could create without limit. Though the public initially found plastic to be tacky, targeted advertisements helped shift perception through promises of sterility and convenience. These tiny wishes for convenience compounded; people began to desire the simplicity of using something and never touching it again. We have begun taking for granted how bizarre it is to have manmade materials wrapped around everything we touch. Our throwaway culture has taught us that, with enough money, we can afford to buy a new toaster if ours breaks. We no longer need the hassle of fixing toasters or cleaning dishes. Our perfect beach day picnic consists of an entire meal that we can throw away when finished—dishes and all.

On the flip side, we've begun equating sustainability with class. If you eat at a five-star restaurant, it is highly likely you'll be eating with real cutlery, real dishes, and even a real cloth napkin. When flying first class, one way airlines make the experience "classier" is to give their elite real, reusable dishes. We want the convenience of never needing to wash a dish, yet we recognize that there is something inherently less refined about single-use goods.

At the end of a flight, I tend to find myself in a rather morose headspace. As the plane circles closer to the ground, I see the huge swaths of ground suffocated in concrete. I am struck by the massive city I'm landing in, the 1.5 million people crammed into this small section of earth wedged between two rivers. I think about how these rivers flow into the ocean. I think about how last year I went scuba diving innumerable times and found garbage during at least 50% of those dives. I wonder how many of the 1.5 million people in my city think about the ocean. I wonder how I can encourage them to do that. I'm overwhelmed and, quite simply, sad.

I doubt anyone with significant environmental knowledge would claim that "skipping the straw" will save the world, but that's not the point. We can't stop a detrimental environmental cascade by removing one piece of single-use plastic from our daily consumption of single-use coffee lids, smoothie cups, sterility wrappers, to-go containers, and more. We can, however, highlight charismatic sea creatures that remind people that the world is so much larger than any one person. The straws I've used may not have wound up in a turtle's nose, but each one I've used in my lifetime is certainly still floating around the planet somewhere. This problem starts small and quickly grows to be astronomical—I like to think that the solution might grow that way too.

ॐ

Christina Stefan is a design researcher with a passion for understanding how people learn and interact. She loves exploring the conservation world to see how design can be used to foster healthy human-nature interactions.

Bio-retrograde-able

J.B. Stone

/ the hue of the sky is still urine yellow / even after the
sun has risen / charcoal lumps of dust / clog the air / like
arteries / clotted vitals / the tint of the open sea is still dark
olive green / even after tides wash away the roots of kelp /
the beds of sargasso / the waves that were once a breeding
ground for sound / now a song muted by abrupt timelines
/ now the fall / soon the landing / in which we pay witness
/ rather than respect / in which we look back / instead of
move forward /

ALONG THE SHORES OF THE ERIE CANAL

J.B. Stone

the portrait of degradation
is constantly painted here

the image of god
is best depicted as a head

peeking from a discolored cloud atlas
nodding in disdain for its children

the only fish in these waters
are always floating

never swimming
never feeding

the only growth in these waters
is always algae

never the lilacs
never the reeds

& the barges are still being updated,
the rust continues to wall away at the landscape

the sludge continues to funnel
into the mouths of Great Lakes waterways

the word *abyss* starts to slowly define
the view from every pier

lighthouses morph into oil rigs
whirlpool quarry descends into a chasm of fractal fault
lines

humanity replaces overpopulated cemeteries
with bodies of water

& the flooded plains
become the new resting place

for life brought to the brink
of ignorance   and then pushed over

J.B. Stone is a neurodivergent writer from Brooklyn, now
residing in Buffalo. Stone is the author of *A Place Between
Expired Dreams and Renewed Nightmares* (Ghost City Press,
2018) and the forthcoming *Fireflies & Hand Grenades* (Stasia
Press, 2019). His reviews, poetry, and prose have appeared
or are forthcoming in *Yes Poetry, Gravel, Five 2 One Magazine,
BlazeVOX, Glass, Empty Mirror, Crack the Spine,* and elsewhere.
Check out more of his work at www.jaredbenjaminstone.
com_or his tweets @JB_StoneTruth.

So This is Starrigavin

Kersten Christianson

The ocean on the western side,
estuary to the east. Paved road
meanders across the bridge, like
a grandfather with an old story

to unpack. A walking path flanks
the road, gathers broken bits
of mussel shells, deer vertebrae,
alder cones. Because it is spring,

green spruce pollen marks pavement
in galactic splatters. Beard lichen
drapes above your head, whispy
to your fingertips when you stretch.

There are crows, ravens, & kingfishers.
Great blue herons fish the tidal zone
shallows, their beady eyes intent, hunting
darting salmon fry at their feet.

So this is Starrigavin. An afternoon walk
with a bag of oyster crackers in your hand
to feed inquisitive corvidae. You push
into the wind, it lifts your hair to join

fluttering beard moss and you swear,
you swear you could lift your arms,
transformed wings, join the feathered,
and fly.

Up the Coast from the Astrolabe

Kersten Christianson

We first stumbled upon Long Point on the arrow-shaped Port au Port Peninsula of Newfoundland via Google Maps from our clunky desktop at home in Alaska. One month later, our own compass arrow draws us first south and then further east, arching north from one rocky island to another, past the treasured astrolabe in Port-Aux-Basque and onward to shore's end.

This day, we bumped our way down twenty-three kilometers of gravel road to the end of Long Point's narrowing, narrower, narrow spit. Eerily quiet, the ancient rocks and eroding cliffs slide into the Gulf of St. Lawrence.

The wind howls, as it often does in this otherwise silent place, forlorn and lonely, but this day of our arrival is warm and the afternoon sun shines in our eyes.

Land of limestone, shale, and sandstone is pocked with empty, dilapidated seasonal fishing shacks perched on the shoreline, and littered with various burn piles of fishermen's belongings left behind (burned out toolbox, bottle of dish soap, flannel shirt).

There are five fishing boats tied to a working dock, but no captains or crews.

A woman, young girl, and small dog exit suddenly from between a row of shacks, dart by with uncertain eye contact. They skirt up the cliffs and disappear into the rock formations like the fog that rolls in without warning.

Wooden lobster pots are piled five high and thirty-five deep on land; airy vessels of netted, dried starfish and urchins, and the countless bright buoys of others at work dot the coastline and bob in the waves, their lines sinking into the deep blue of the day.

We examine fossilized rocks imprinted with the signatures of ancient ocean dwellers, namely trilobites, and collect worn wood pieces, knotted rope, and shells to haul home for winter beading projects.

I think of this afternoon in time-lapse. Certainly, this place has heard the lilting cadence of French and Basque languages, the first notes of a fiddle removed from a battered case; the old songs and stories of fine catch and sea disasters around a crackling bonfire; perhaps even the laughter of the little girl who disappeared into the rock.

ACHE

Kersten Christianson

For the suckerhole
of lantern light, brilliant sun
spotlighting ocean;
Herkimer, yellow jasper
skip along a midnight sea.

༚

Kersten Christianson is a raven-watching, moon-gazing Alaskan. When not exploring the summer lands and dark winter of the Yukon, she lives in Sitka, Alaska. She holds an MFA in Creative Writing (University of Alaska Anchorage). Kersten has authored two books of poetry: *What Caught Raven's Eye* (Petroglyph Press, 2018) and *Something Yet to Be Named* (Aldrich Press, 2017). Her newest collection, *Curating the House of Nostalgia* (Sheila-Na-Gig Editions, 2020), will be released in June. She is also the poetry editor of the quarterly journal *Alaska Women Speak*, and can be reached at www.kerstenchristianson.com.

SUBMERGING

Anthony Panegyres

The veins on Grandpa's legs protruded like thick tidal lines. Sam and Caleb scrambled to catch up, their toes vanishing and reappearing in the chalky sand as they trailed him homewards. Sam stared up at the island's cliff, its base gnawed away by the climbing ocean, leaving only a thin shelf. Other places were submerging too: the jetty where he had nearly caught that white sea-snake was completely under.

I would have brought it in, jeweled skin glittering silver and white, if only they'd let me.

Once home, Sam and Caleb sunk into their beanbags and watched *Family Guy* as the aroma of stewing fish, breadfruit, and coconut milk wafted out from Grandpa's kitchen.

This was the family; Dad did not count, not anymore. He had nicked off to Brisbane. Their two aunts lived in New Zealand and never visited. Sam remembered his Grandpa's words: "Everyone runs away."

Caleb will leave. All his brother spoke of was Queensland and the trip their dad had taken them on. Those adventure parks where the mad rides were higher than any dune they had ever run down; the flash cars that purred; the beach girls that came in every colour.

Tavloa is a paradise—it just needs some care. It was their place and their island and their ocean.

"Sam! Caleb!" hollered Grandpa. "Set the table."

The boys placed cutlery and bowls out on the small pine table that still managed to saturate the kitchen space.

"Grouper today, boys." Grandpa ladled the steaming stew out before them and clasped his ocean-scarred hands together. "Thank you, Christ our Lord, for our dinner, and take care of our ancestors." They crossed themselves and dug into the large fish, which was good, soft, and flaky white. A change too—usually they used those finicky finer nets for tiny ones, like baitfish. "Just got to adapt, I guess," Grandpa would say. "Lil'uns are tasty. But years ago there was big fish everywhere." He'd gesture, as did all fisherman, spreading his arms to indicate size. "Those ships way out've scooped 'em up and the lil'uns have grown crazy with fewer big 'uns to eat 'em."

Ordinarily, Sam could not wait for Sunday. Tomorrow was when everyone gathered outside the town hall after church. They would gorge themselves on pigs off the spit, crunching on the salty crackle and then tearing into the white meat beneath as the juice and fat dribbled down their lips and over their fingers.

But tomorrow was the dance.

Sam stared at his plate.

"You'll get it too, Sam," said Grandpa. "Just be strong, be patient."

Caleb laughed. Sam jabbed his brother in the rib.

"Hey! I didn't mean nothin'."

Sam gripped his fork and stabbed down at some pale flesh on his plate. *It isn't right. My arms slap the wrong places.* He often hid away behind the rusted goat shed and practised until his feet felt heavier than iron, but his body did not respond like the other boys'. Disobedient knees buckled when he spread them; his shoulders slid when they should tremble.

They washed the dishes, then sat at the table as Grandpa

warmed some goat's milk on the stove. He unwrapped a bowl next to him, revealing two mangrove crabs already painted red by boiling water, and brought them to the table. Caleb grabbed a claw and pretended to cut his wrist off.

"We'll eat 'em tomorrow night," said Grandpa. "We only had one or two of these ever when I was a boy. Didn't really have a mangrove swamp back then. Caught six today, gave two away, and sold the other couple."

"They're massive," said Sam.

"You boys be careful down 'em mangroves. Could really snap your hand off there, Caleb."

Sam picked up a crab, rapped the hard shell, and gingerly touched the spikes where the joints were.

"Remember to take a long stick to test for bogs around the groves. Some of that mud sinks dangerously. You'll do your part to grow that swamp on the east side and plant 'em mangrove trees to keep the ocean back."

Grandpa's talk of the mangroves and combating the ocean was an echo the boys had heard time and again.

While they sipped their milk, Grandpa told a tale of an ancestor who called turtles to the boat. It was said he would feed the entire village in a single outing.

"One day, however . . ." His voice became hushed. "He called too many, and turtles of all kinds—leatherbacks, greens, browns—leapt from the water onto the craft. Their shells cuttin' into calves and feet. Others yelled at him to stop, eventually pushin' 'im down and wrappin' their hands round his mouth, but it was too late, they kept leapin' on board until the craft sunk, drownin' the Turtle Caller and all the crew. Some say they're still on that ocean bed, and, if you fish that spot, you'll know 'cause you can still hear his ghost callin' for 'em turtles."

The boys shared the mattress, feet to head.

"You'll be okay tomorrow," said Caleb. "It's just a dance."

"Yeah," Sam said as he lay there, sleeplessly awaiting the grey light of dawn.

A throng of people gathered around the three pigs smoking on spits in the foyer of the whitewashed hall. The boys formed two lines with gaps so that everyone could see. It would be better if the girls weren't watching; their brown eyes swallowed him. Grandpa, with an encouraging smile, stood behind Seth, the instructor. Sam imagined Seth as his grandpa's younger reflection. Muscular, able.

Caleb turned around in front of him with a wink that said it'd be fine. When they began the chant, Sam felt okay as his first knee bent, but then the smoke from the spits floated over, almost choking him. He lost rhythm. Seth called a halt.

"Sam, hit that leg, let your knee tremble, and your body will follow."

"It's the smoke." His voice quavered.

"Don't blame the smoke. Watch." And Seth shifted from one bent knee to the other, his chest shaking in response. "See?"

Sam gulped some phlegm and fought to hold back tears. There was too much shame in crying.

They started again. In the background, fat dripped onto the coals, striking it in sharp sizzles. The air was heavy, leaden in the heat. Once more, he missed the step. Everything buzzed. Sounds blurred and amplified: the laughter, the hissing and crackling, the dull thud of their feet on the pavement. He hung his head. His eyes watered a little, surely from the smoke. He was not some cry-baby.

He pushed past one dancer, then another and another. Girls pointed at him; the crowd pointed, too, as he shoved his way clear through them all.

"Sam!" Grandpa called.

Grandpa wouldn't catch him. Only Sam's toes hit the ground as he sprinted through the village. Past the few tiny shops joined together by common walls. Past the sole asphalt road and the fenceless homes with overgrown beach shrubs. His mind emptied as the wind cooled his face and his heart drove blood to all parts of his body. He held his head straight and pumped his muscles, even when his calves ached and his thighs trembled.

Once out of the village he still ran, now more measured. *One, two. One, two.* At the slower pace he thought of isolated places. *The caves? Too damp. Too dark. The beaches? Too open.* He decided on the mangroves. *This is my island. No one can steal it from me. Not the dance, not the rising ocean, not my father in Brisbane, and not the people drawn to the mainland that blinds them.*

One, two, one, two. Across the island he ran. Around the small bracken lake that had held fresh water in his grandpa's youth. Past the scrubland and the crumbling house of some former English governor. He ran until his breath wheezed and all that could move him were the numbers: *one, two, one, two, one, two.* He reached the swamp's outskirts, jogged for a while before entering the shallows. As the foggy water sprayed his ankles, he did not feel the midges and sand flies, or see the mudskippers hop away, or notice the crabs retreating with their pincers raised.

The wind between the swamp trees sounded like the faint singing of old ladies who knew all the hymns. Soon he was in a world of shadow, mangrove branches above him, occasional blades of light piercing gaps between the trees. Standing cormorants, their prehistoric wings held out to dry, flew from him whenever he neared.

He'd go deeper, out to where the bogs stopped and you could swim if you were gutsy enough. But his feet sunk, plunging him up to his calves in mud. He made to move and it swept up higher. Again he stirred and, this time, it climbed to his knees.

Be still. That way it'll take longer to sink. Move, and no one will arrive in time.

He yelled, a wordless noise. If anyone were searching for him, they would be a while yet.

To stem his breathing rate, he counted the air in and out.

His thoughts fled briefly to hopes of a vague future. To finding a wife who wanted to stay on the island; to becoming a fisherman like Grandpa and a better family man than his dad.

The mud rose slightly, concealing his knees. He yelled once more. This time his mind sank into the past, as if the mud laid claim to him.

Sam remembered fragments from as far back as four. His mother, with eyes like warm coals and hair that fell in waves like the night ocean. He remembered when they all slept together, sandwiched on that same bed, with Grandpa alone in the other room.

He remembered the UN men who came with countless sandbags, instructing the islanders where and how to lay them to keep the ocean back. Sam could recall their words but only one face: John's, a Welsh UN officer with a mop of red curls and a moustache that flamed down his face to his chin.

"Nice place," John said, and his lagoon-like eyes gazed at

Sam's mother. Sam, even then, knew something was askew, and grabbed his mother's hand to lead her away. But their eyes stuck like the eyes of competitors. Who knew where they disappeared to on the island? His mother abandoned them all for Wales soon after. He wanted more from her than farewell, more than tears.

The mud gradually crept up to his thighs. By the time Sam was five, his father, defeated, no longer fished with Grandpa. He became flabby, like a seal. It was Grandpa who allowed Dad to leave. When they came into the house that afternoon, it had reeked of that overly sweet stench of coconut left to rot. Dad had not cleaned at all but sat by the tinny radio, listening to the stories of others. Grandpa switched the machine off. Dad stood up, swung at Grandpa and missed. Another side of Grandpa unveiled itself as the old man's hand snaked out and grabbed his son's throat. Dad's cheeks turned the colour of a bruise as Grandpa spoke.

"Don't let this hurt swallow your life."

The mud climbed, tickling Sam's testicles. "Help!" he screamed as loud as his lungs permitted.

He recalled his obsession with his teacher, Miss Rodanui, in Year Three. Drawing attention to himself by leaping onto a desk in class and reciting the opening of a "Revolting Rhyme" by Roald Dahl. He remembered those stinking, hot days. Sandy-coloured grass, no breeze, giant hornets terrifying them. He trailed her around the tire-swings in the dirt playground to hear her voice and glimpse her face.

Muck seeped up to his nipples.

He remembered rafting with Caleb, way out past the breakers. The wind turned, slapping the raft, stirring the water. Shadowy clouds jostled overhead. They toppled and were caught in the white foam, twirling. Sam's arms thrashed until he found the raft's edge. He clambered aboard with a splutter and heaved Caleb—who was gripping the raft—back on as blood streamed from a gash in his brother's head into the ocean, where it stained parts of the water a powdery red.

It neared his shoulders.

Just off shore: Sampson, the sea lion that mauled everyone's catch but, regardless, was loved by all. Stingrays, which they handfed in the shallows, moving like dark ponds over the ocean bed. The white sea-snake that he wanted to bring in off the guano-stained jetty, but they'd cut his line.

"Let me bring it in," he'd called out as others around him laughed, making him feel red.

Let me bring it in. Those words recurred in his mind over and over as the mud reached his forming Adam's apple. Briny rivulets fled from his eyes, he lifted his head and shouted— or sobbed—repeatedly,

"Let me bring it in! Let me bring it in!"

There were voices in the distance. Sam looked over, his throat raw, his body ensnared.

Grandpa and Caleb trudged through sludge on the far side of the bog. *Is there time?* Perhaps if there was, even with the jetty long since drowned, he would bring that ivory serpent in.

☙

Since 2011 Anthony Panegyres (a PhD candidate at University of Western Australia) has been an Aurealis Award Finalist for Best Fantasy Short Story and has had stories published in Australia's premier literary journals, including *Meanjin* and twice in *Overland*, as well as several anthologies, including *The Best Australian Stories*, *The Year's Best Asutralian Fantasy & Horror, 2011 & 2015*. His latest stories can be found in the anthologies *Bloodlines* and *At the Edge*, and in 2019: *We'll Stand in That Place and Other Stories* and *The Sky Falls Down: An Anthology of Loss*.

"Submerging" was originally published in *Overland* 214 and was republished in *The Best Australian Stories* 2014 and *The Sky Falls Down: An Anthology of Loss*

POSTCARDS FROM MY FUTURE SELF: BEVERLY BEACH, FLORIDA

Sheree Winslow

Never turn your back on the ocean. Every time you go to the beach—every single time—your mom repeats the warning: one of the first things she learned when she moved to California. You think she overlearned the rule, but when you camp on the beach with her in Florida, she lets down her guard while floating in the warm Atlantic, turns toward shore just before a large wave strikes, sweeps designer prescription sunglasses off her face into the revolving churn. She mopes for days that she didn't follow her own advice, angry to be mugged by the water. The memory ebbs and flows in your mind as you watch news reports: waves grow bigger and bigger, storms flex stronger and stronger. Scientists analyze how much time we have until the impact of climate change is catastrophic. Hurricane Michael flattens Mexico Beach, claims homes and possessions and lives, leaves survivors nothing. Islands of garbage swirl around containers fallen from ships—just because we want more and more stuff. Young soldiers die in wars fought over oil. Wildlife suffer spills in Alaska and the Gulf. We turn our faces inward, suspended in the warmth of denial. We consume more than we need, ignoring the swell at our backs.

❧

Given the name Many-Trails-Many-Roads-Woman by the medicine man of her Northern Cheyenne tribe, Sheree Winslow embraces a life of wonder and wander. She's the 2018 recipient of the Submittable Eliza So fellowship, among other honors. Her work has recently appeared or is forthcoming in *Midway Journal*, **82 Review*, *Beecher's*, *Linea*, *Past Ten*, *Wanderlust*, *Brevity*, *The Sun Reader's Write*, *AWP Writer's Notebook*, *Mom Egg Review*, *Memoir Magazine*, and *Storm Cellar*. Sheree lives in Southern California where she's finishing a memoir about recovery from food addiction and a collection of travel reflections while advising startup and marketing clients. She received her MFA from Vermont College of Fine Arts.

STATE OF THE EARTH: WHAT'S TO SHOW FOR OURSELVES

Gerard Sarnat

Blazing Hyperion on his orbed fire
Still sat, still snuff'd the incense, teeming up
From man to the sun's God; yet unsecure:
For as among us mortals omens drear
Fright and perplex, so also shuddered he—

John Keats

Union hunkered for storms to pass,
I stumble on the UK's Daily Mail headline:
"Meet Hyperion: Largest structure
ever found in the early universe
is one million, billion times
more massive than the sun."

While the more constructive of Post-WWII's
Boomer Generation (me included) spouted
sunny revolutionary rhetoric about how to create
A Great American Dream Machine,
all we made was a Great Pacific Garbage Patch
—nightmare twice the size of Texas.

Less solid, ore gyre swirling in winds and currents,
the vast carrousel of toothbrushes, bottles, umbrella
handles, toy guns, jerricans, laundry baskets never stops

—but what's worse are the tons of ghost nets abandoned by fishermen which ensnare seals, sea turtles, us.

૭૦

Notes: *The Daily Mail* headline refers to an article written by Cheyenne MacDonald, 17 October 2018. Another article mentioned in the poem was published 4 February 2019 in New Yorker magazine by Carolyn Kormann, titled "A Grand Plan to Clean the Great Pacific Garbage Patch."

Gerard Sarnat is a physician who's built and staffed homeless clinics, as well as a Stanford University professor and healthcare CEO. He won the Poetry in the Arts First Place Award plus the Dorfman Prize, and has been nominated for Pushcarts plus Best of the Net Awards. Gerry is published in academic-related journals from institutions including Stanford, Oberlin, Brown, Columbia, Virginia Commonwealth, Harvard, Johns Hopkins, Wesleyan, and the University of Edinburgh.

Gerry's writing has also appeared widely, including such U.S. outlets as *Gargoyle, Main Street Rag, New Delta Review, Blue Mountain Review, Brooklyn Review, San Francisco Magazine, The Los Angeles Review*, and *The New York Times*. Pieces have also been accepted by Chinese, Bangladeshi, Hong Kongese, Singaporian, Canadian, English, Irish, Scotch, Australian, New Zealander, French, German, Indian, Israeli, Swedish and Fijian publications. *Kaddish for the Country* was selected for pamphlet distribution nationwide on Inauguration Day 2016. *Amber Of Memory* was chosen for the 50th Harvard reunion Dylan symposium. Gerry has also authored the collections *Homeless Chronicles* (2010), *Disputes* (2012), *17s* (2014), and *Melting the Ice King* (2016).

SLICK

Julie Wilson

Some birds' beauty
comes from iridescence,
the play of light revealing
changing colours buried
in black feathers.

Don't be misled.

Any bird that swims
the rainbows
of this congealed sea
will find not beauty

but death.

৵

Juliet Wilson is a writer, crafter, adult education tutor, and conservation volunteer based in Edinburgh, UK. She blogs at www.craftygreenpoet.blogspot.com and tweets @ craftygreenpoet.

EULOGY FOR A WHALE

Franciszka Voletz

after you washed up several times
emaciated and distressed
off the coast of Norway
euthanization seemed the only option
and when they looked inside
this is what they found:
over thirty plastic bags of varying sizes
and other manufactured trash
matted in your stomach
blocking your intestines

the whale's digestive system
was completely depleted of nutrients
said terje lislevand, a zoologist and professor
who worked with a team on your necropsy
they discovered:
candy wrappers, bread bags, a potato chip bag,
along with countless bits of small plastics
in addition to the trash and grocery bags
that they later laid out flat on the concrete

if i could have sung the suffering
out of your spirit, i would have
even if it meant beginning the song now
(sending sound to carry you through wave after wave)
and making it the aria that never ends

Note: The world economic forum reports that each year, at least eight million tons of plastics leak into the ocean (equivalent to dumping the contents of one garbage truck into the ocean every minute). The best research currently available estimates that there are over 150 million tons of plastics in the ocean today. In a business-as-usual scenario, the ocean is expected to contain one ton of plastic for every three tons of fish by 2025, and by 2050, more plastics than fish (by weight).

Pouring the Prayer

Franciszka Voletz

this thirst brings us together gathering around
a spill, the cool dribble, this trickle stored
in blasphemous vessels bound to break to bits
brittling in the guts of gulls, the GI tracts of salmon
while whales wash and wash ashore

their weakened bodies
ushering in the panic, the mobilization
the muscle-sore work
to turn them right, to send them back

but they keep signaling

with their barnacled flesh with their
fatigued fins with their plastic-filled intestines and
bone-shaped ribs showing through thick skin
they keep drifting in

towards tireless humans pouring
bucket by bucket the water over and over and over them
pouring the prayer, pouring the sheen back
over oceanblacked skin
pouring the prayer that they might thrive
that they might make another great migration
that they, that we, that they might make it
that they, that we, that they might be ok

OCEAN / ASHTRAY

Franciszka Voletz

the heave and sway of swells
washing, a blue frothing, a rushing in
how the tides roll and crash
swish and gush
surge and sweep
each drift and swirl
of water on water on salt on water
a magnificent and pounding thunder
the sheen of sun on surface
a glint as good as gold

diving in dirty
we walk out clean
skin that sings
it's cellular
all the way through
skin and muscle to bone

this gift of deliverance
offered again and again
carried on effervescent crests
smacking all the old
off slack flesh

and what is it we bring you:
our nicotine-stained offerings
our cellulose acetate
cigarette butts
afloat in your froth
spun in your undulations
pummeled to shreds
pulled out to sea
washed in
and carried out again

who taught us
to give this kind of thanks
who taught us
this sin of separateness

છે

Note: The number one human-made contaminant in the world's oceans is cigarette butts—they also rank as the most littered item in the world. Cigarette filters are made from cellulose acetate—a form of plastic—and used butts contain hundreds of chemicals used to treat tobacco.

Sources:
Ocean Conservancy. *International Coastal Cleanup 2017 Report.* Ocean Conservancy 2017.
Truth Initiative. *Tobacco and the Environment.* 2018.

A Spell For Healing A Favorite Body Of Water

Franciszka Voeltz

lie the length of your body
along the length of its body
sand grit pressing to forearms and calves
sun-soaked stones melting anything hard in you

unlace yourself and follow its shifting shore
the skin of your arches telling you
about brittle twigs and water-washed feathers

press your hands
to its ferned and mossed banks
touch the roots that grab hold there

find a way to talk about it
without using the word it

watch the movement—
circles concentric-ing out
along a glassy surface
whitewater rushing
over a tumble of rocks
or the curls of tidal surges
as they roll and roll

sink your fingers into
the cool shock or

sun warmed swells
contemplate your blood, your cells, your marrow
consider
how you and the water
are made of each other

lower your whole self in if possible,
air tracing edges of uncovered skin
offer your heartbeat
to the molecules that move wet around you
and whisper
may you heal
may you thrive
may you be whole

if you can't reach the water
then lean in, close as you can
and listen like you would listen
to a lover's heart, ear pressed to chest

if you can't get close
then simply turn to face the water's direction
and call
like a hawk to her young
or sing like mandolin strings
or just hum quietly
for all the power water has
to clean
to kill
to bring life
face it and say
thank you

in whatever way
you know how:
a gesture
a word
an offering

promise your beloved water body
you will tend to it
in whatever ways you are capable
(bring a bag
for collecting trash)

practice beholding any water
you come across
the same way you would behold
a rattlesnake
poised to strike in your path

it is all
holy

❧

Franciszka Voeltz received an MFA in Writing from the University of California at San Diego. Her chapbook *All This Blue, All This Broken* is available from Iron Point Press, and her work has appeared in journals including *Adrienne*, *Dark Mountain*, and *Analecta Literary Journal*. She has received poetry fellowships from the Helene Wurlitzer Foundation, Santa Fe Art Institute, Brush Creek Foundation for the Arts, and Art Farm.

EUBALAENA GLACIALIS

D'Ores & Deja

It's not the swish of rainfall over water
or the comforting crash

of wave on rock. It's not the pop
gun of snapping

shrimp in shallow waters or the dolphins
and the echo of their clever

chatter. It's not the grind of colliding
icebergs as they shatter.

It is stillness lost to ships, their persistent
rumble. It is the seismic

explorations that muffle the languid pulse
of our mating calls.

It is the way our songs became so crude,
censored by the shrieking

sonar. And it is here, in the heaviness of air,
that silence surfaces again.

ॐ

Writing and photography duo d'Ores&Deja live and work in the former Tar Gardens of the Amsterdam harbor area. The Dutch-French duo formed in June of last year. Their work has recently appeared in *The London Reader* and *Antiphon*.

Seasons of Sunken Hydrophones

Mandy-Suzanne Wong

Bermuda dwindled to a pallid line like a whisper of cloud above the ocean's ponderous blue. Profound blue, admitting nothing, deferring sunlight in hard twinkles all the way to Antarctica. Captain cut the engine almost fifteen miles offshore. We'd crossed a canyon none of us could see, sunk in 1,220 meters of water. We bobbed like a bottlecap in the vicinity of the sea mountain Challenger.

Couldn't see that either. Or discern its conical shape fifty meters down. Challenger, like the great horn of the gramophone. Later, Andrew Stevenson told me—Andrew was the one in the little boat off to starboard—Challenger is a giant "echo chamber," a grand acoustic resonator.

So we waited.

Seven Northern Atlantic humpback whales heard our boats from leagues away. Monolithic heads dotted with barnacles rose out of the water almost close enough to touch. And the deep eyes looked at us.

They were on their spring migration from the Caribbean, where, in winter, calves are born, to the cold waters of Labrador. There they'd feast and spend the summer, turn around in autumn to socialize off Hispaniola, then do it all again. Bermuda's seamounts are a stop on the way.

Not always. Each whale has a favorite route. Some zigzag up to Canada so they can visit Challenger. Some linger around the mountain for weeks on end. A notable few skip the Caribbean and winter here. Since 2007, Andrew's identified over 1,500 unique humpback visitors to Bermuda. Several hundred individuals return again and again. They're the reason Andrew wooed the makers of the AMAR.

Autonomous Multichannel Acoustic Recorder: a gray log nearly as tall as I, containing up to eight hydrophones and 1,700 GB of solid-state memory. It's the sort of thing they use to listen for submarines. After convincing various governments that he isn't a spy, in April of 2018, Andrew hooked an AMAR pair to custom buoys and sent them down forty-three meters to Challenger's summit. With luck, they'd stay there through the winter.

Hydrophone art has awesome subversive potential. Consider the technology's history.

Boston, 1901. The microphone Thomas Edison developed for early telephones is stuffed into a watertight container. In all subsequent wars involving Western powers, submarines are all the rage, so hydrophones are too. Until the 1990s, Bermuda's waters are peppered with US naval hydrophones listening for Japanese and Russian subs, the idea being to torpedo them. The hydrophone is a war machine. Like the radio and tape recorder.

Today anyone can buy one. Andrew used a consumer-grade hydrophone at first, dangling it from his boat with the cables in his hands, listening for whales and dolphins so he could wander closer to them and film them.

He no longer uses hydrophones for that. "I don't chase after [whales]," Andrew says. "I go to the right area [where whales often congregate], but I will sit there and not move, basically wait for the whales to come to me." And so he waits. He listens with naked ears; humpback song is loud enough to shake the hull of the boat. He watches the horizon, strains for a glimpse of telltale lobs or blows. And waits.

Sometimes for a whole season.

Back in 2010, Andrew used snippets of his hydrophone recordings in his award-winning documentary *Where the Whales Sing.* (It shows Bermuda's hands bloodied in the early whaling industry, the ocean soiled with today's pollutants and fishing nets.) But why use only snippets if humpbacks sing so sweetly? Because, for Andrew, recording isn't a hunt for aesthetic resources. He records nonhuman voices because listening is an important part of loving. He upgraded to a military-grade AMAR for the same reason.

A technology of death. Re-envisioned and upcycled to attend to alien life.

The first recordings of humpback sounds were accidents.

Because St. David's is the closest Bermuda gets to Russia, the US Navy planted hydrophones in the water off St. David's. In the 1950s and '60s, the hydrophones connected via cable to the office of Frank Watlington, a Bermuda-born engineer and hydrophone designer. He heard a lot of whoops and moans.

Submarines don't moan. So Watlington took out his binoculars. He saw the geyser of a humpback's blow right above the hydrophones.

As late as 1952, humans had no idea what they heard when they heard humpbacks. Watlington was one of the first to connect humpback sounds with humpback whales. He gave the tapes to an American biologist to make sure whaling companies couldn't get hold of them. This biologist, Roger Payne, "had the guts to include the b word" in his analysis.

The *b* word is *beauty*. From Watlington's recordings and a couple of his own, Payne produced the 1970 multiplatinum sensation *Songs of the Humpback Whale*. 10 million *National Geographic* readers each received a copy.

Five untreated recordings of humpback whales. No drums, no strums. Just whales. No layering, no more reverb than is natural 450 meters down.

"I had never heard anything like it... Tears flowed from our cheeks," recalled Katy Payne, a musician and biologist who was among the first to hear Watlington's tapes. "The sounds were so beautiful, so powerful, so variable. And as we eventually learned, [the sounds of the famous 'Solo Whale'] were all the products of one singing animal—one animal." Payne was the first to hear a connection between the methodical structures of humpback sounds and the elaborate arrangements of certain primate sounds. Listening to whales, "by golly," she heard music.

Songs delivered an earthquake to Western popular cultures. The story of the album's incredible influence on all kinds of music, dance, Hollywood media, even space exploration has been told again and again. From its intense emotional impact on so many, the "Save The Whales" movement was born, and whaling was outlawed in several countries. All this sprang from a military accident on a tiny island.

Andrew wants to do it again. This time on purpose.

Not the multiplatinum business. He's not in it for that. Not since Watlington has anyone recorded humpback sounds over an extended period with military-grade equipment in the crystal waters of said tiny island. Andrew's just in it to listen. To learn how migrant whales are faring in today's sick and screaming Atlantic.

❧

In 2009, a humpback turned his tail up to the sky, his nose to the crown of Challenger seamount. He hung there for twenty-three minutes. Andrew recorded him with the "engine off, the hydrophone about 30 feet down in 170 feet of water." The audio of this whale sounding out his whaliness is available on Andrew's YouTube channel. No one's seen him since, so Andrew never nicknamed him. I call him Exile.

"I believe there are some whales that sing more beautifully than others, and this recording struck us as being particularly good," Andrew wrote. "We hear the humpbacks singing often in this exact location," often with several whales "milling around the singer." And they're not singing for sex; their conduct simply "is not the aggressive behavior seen in the [Caribbean or Hawaiian] breeding grounds." Having filmed two male humpbacks dancing tenderly together, and radically hypothesizing that some postmenopausal humpback grandmothers sing and compose songs, Andrew knows that whales aren't mere puppets of evolution.

Certain individuals, like Exile, cultivate truly enviable artistic talents.

But nowadays, the thought of listening to people like Exile makes bipeds groan. One philosopher thinks anyone who's interested in humpback sound is only interested because there's something wrong with them. Born of "loneliness," "social impoverishment," or a pathological imagination, an "interest in cetaceans was a direct response to the unlivability of modern life, serving as 'the nostalgic imaginary of postindustrial culture.'" Another scholar adds that liking whale song is for "hippies, best known as popular purveyors of environmentalist values (harmony, one-ness, etc.)" who want "a blissful escape from the worries of the day."

Even fellow field recordists like David Michael, whose recording of humans shooting a cow and trying to justify themselves with religious sermons gained some notoriety, complains that there's no "sign of man" in *Songs of the Humpback*. "That's unrealistic nowadays," Michael says. No matter where we go, we'll hear ourselves or our machines; to think otherwise is "pastoral," pure "fantasy." And not naive fantasy but arrogant denial. Anthropocentric, capitalistic denial encourages humans to forget that we thrive at the expense of immeasurable nonhuman suffering.

But there are places we can't touch. Challenger is full of caves too deep for us, unexplored except by the nonhumans who live there. I think that's only right. Oceans are not our empires. Oceans aren't liquid slaughterhouses or oil reservoirs. Oceans live. But not for us.

Art can sound this out, help us learn it with our bodies, make it emotional. When artworks make us *feel* that nonhuman animals are not us and not for us, those artworks do something very necessary. So especially in deep-sea recordings, I don't think it's fantastical to hear our absence. I think it's appropriate. *Not* hearing humans in *Songs of the Humpback Whale* undercuts the ideological fantasy that humans are the center of the universe, having colonized absolutely everything. Technical details aside, the album's critical edge is its listening for human absence in a place humans should leave alone. Leaving the ocean alone isn't "blissful harmony" but shutting up already.

Watlington didn't edit humans out of his recordings. He simply left them out. He recorded "Solo Whale," the best-known track on *Songs* and, for many years, the longest

humpback sound sequence ever recorded, 457 meters underwater in 1960s St. David's. No human could dive to 457
meters in the 1960s, and in St. David's, no one did. That
part of the island saw little water traffic. It was closed to
all Bermudians except those working for the US Navy. So
Watlington's project wasn't like those wildlife films where
we never see the camera crew because they're staging the
illusion that humans have transcended "Nature," leaving it
"pristine." He just recorded where humans weren't. Why?
Because that's where the US wanted their top-secret hydrophones. Since Watlington had to listen from shore via cable,
his own presence was impossible for the hydrophones to
capture. My point is, some whales really sing where humans
can't get at them. And that's a good thing.

Anyway, heaven forbid that when we listen to whales,
we listen to whales. Listen not for where *we* are but for *their*
voices. For their sakes.

Talk of humans listening to humpbacks out of hubristic
delusions or as some kind of narcotic assumes that listening to whales *just to listen to whales* is impossible. As though
whales were doomed unto extinction to serve as resources
for human psychological consumption. If humpback whales
once filled our corsets with their bones, our umbrellas with
their baleen—if sperm whales lit our homes with the nasal
oil that should've made their voices heard across the globe—
now it's like the only reason we'd pay them any attention
would be to fill our sick hearts with their light.

Every recorded sound references something absent. Not
even the humans in Michael's recordings are present when
we hear them except in a ghostly way. But when we take
listening to whales as a sign of our own noxiousness or deign
to care about whales' welfare only insofar as it affects our

own, the whale itself, the living one who does the whooping, is doubly canceled out. We talk over his whaliness. Or ignore it in search of diagnoses for ourselves.

Andrew knows we don't need humpbacks to tell us we're socially impoverished. He hopes his documentaries will inspire humans to care for all ocean life, quit throwing refuse in the water, and stop whaling for real. *Save The Whales* succeeded in illegalizing whaling, but there's this saying about rules... Some countries blatantly ignore the International Whaling Commission. In Greenland, where some of Exile's kinfolk spend the summer, they could still find themselves on the wrong end of a harpoon. From Alaska to Norway to Japan to St. Vincent, harpoons zipping through one loophole or another continue to slaughter whales of all kinds.

The trouble is, nonhumans are nowhere's citizens. If some nation would grant legal citizenship to whales as *persons*, then laws against whale murder would really mean something. Plenty of philosophically-minded humans argue in favor of nonhuman citizenship. In countries like Japan, Spain, New Zealand, and the US, certain human communities have lobbied for the legal rights of dolphins, pets, chimpanzees, and elephants as *persons* instead of "property." But victories against anthropocentric legal systems are rare; for now, wherever they go, nonhuman animals are more like refugees. Humpbacks in particular are lifelong migrants. Perennial visitors. Eternal exiles.

If Andrew's AMAR project has a message, it is this, I think: Whether humpbacks hang around for two weeks or three seasons, they will eventually leave. They're as transient as the tides. To be a whale is to belong to nobody, to elude

51

every clutch. Like we cannot clutch at springtime, so we cannot grasp the secrets of the seamount fathoms deep.

At least that's how it *should* be, being a whale. It's the human realms, obsessed with categorization, which decree that if you don't belong, you don't deserve protection.

The AMARs couldn't leave the mountain. Barbells made sure of it. So they waited. And waited. And maybe they could hear shrimpish chatter and upwellings sweeping up the slopes, parrotfish snip-snipping at the parasites in coralline wrinkles as, nearby, a toadfish grunted. Hear, in all those coincidental differences, the ocean's dearth of borders. Hear humpbacks exfoliate against sandy ledges, nurse their calves, roll in the currents, upturn their flukes to the sky, and bellow compositions to the mountain. Hear Challenger broadcast to the wide ocean; invitations for friends to band together for the trip through orca territory, where so many wounds are opened, so many losses suffered from which the undevoured never heal. Hear, when krill and plankton beckon, the whales' vanishing north.

The AMAR project has no name, for now. But if I could give it one…

The idea of these unmanned listeners waiting, fathoms below, for anyone not human or machine, for anyone at all who might happen along; this idea is beautiful to me whether it's art or not. The solitude of it, the uncertainty, not knowing how it will turn out, whether "it" will turn out to be anything at all. The question of what questions really are addressed by all this effort. And the beauty—how beautiful are fishy clatters and whale songs…

All this sort of thing is the pulse of aesthetic endeavor. When it comes to such things, we don't know why we do them necessarily. But we do them necessarily. Whether or not, in the end, they "mean" anything, whether or not they "make a difference," which we may never know.

I'd call it *three seasons of sunken hydrophones with seamount, upwellings, and migrants who pass and pass and pass.*

For twenty-nine minutes, the AMARs listened at the humpbacks' favorite frequencies (30-4000 Hz). For a minute, their attention wandered into the deep-bass registers of Cuvier's beaked whales. They slept awhile. Then they did it all again in hopes that someone wandered by at just the right time and just the right frequency before the hydrophones' attention wandered. The hydrophones were focused meanderers. Homing in on frequency bands only to abandon them again and again.

It's as if this listening project operated on two timescales at once. One was protracted and slow, the other narrow and fleeting. A single listening moment went on for months on end: the hydrophonic moment, this single recording session stretching on and on as long as it takes to swim to Canada and then Dominica. At the same time, each listening moment was no longer than the hydrophones' attention to a single band. Time as liquid, changing shape. "Oscillating ocean time," one researcher called it. The AMARs listened as the ocean lives. So slowly it seems unchanging. So fast a single wave can dismember a coastline.

Few humans will hear Andrew's AMAR recordings. This troubled me at first, his not making something with the sounds. It's difficult for a human to overcome the ideologically ingrained urge to consume interesting things, take them for ourselves, put them to use somehow.

Imagine an installation where Andrew's three-season recording played continuously, uncut, at all hours of the day and night. Listeners could come and stay like the seamount, or come and go like the fish and the whales; perhaps we'd coincide with the ghost of Exile singing something like the ballad he learned from ancestors and acquaintances, which is all the rage in this oscillating moment. Or we'd listen in on shrimp talk for four days running. Or hear nothing at all unless we waited, waited. Three seasons of a moment of waiting for a coincidence. Whether someone answered our coming with cries, crackles, or cold silences, we'd learn the hope and frustration of migrants; we'd experience only what little we were offered as the whales slip through our fingers.

But Andrew will not use whales' voices as artistic resources. They are not ours for the taking. What they say, who gets to hear it—by rights, none of that is up to us.

&

The whales might overwinter in Bermuda, they might not. Come springtime, they might gather at Challenger, they might not. It's up to them. And it's not. The tides, the moon, krill, orcas, planktonic upwellings. Others decide where and when humpbacks come and go. And not only nonhumans.

"Gulf of Maine" humpbacks are those who'd rather hug the US coast than detour to Bermuda. Yet more and more "Mainers" are changing their migration routes to visit Challenger. Why?

"If the seamounts were being used as gathering points because of the good acoustics, I wondered if the higher proportion of Maine whales coming further out to sea to Bermuda to assemble was because of the noise pollution along the [US] eastern seaboard," Andrew wrote.

Noise pollution.

Container ships, cruise ships, seismic testing, offshore drilling. Above all, war machines. The US military doesn't care that sonar is death to oceanic animals even during training exercises. Sometimes, the US Navy intentionally uses whales for sonar target practice. The victims flee to the surface, struggling to swim with their heads out of the water, blood streaming from their ears. Some beach themselves on purpose, unable to bear it. Others perish from the bends as they surface in a panic.

In Bermuda, whales find cleaner if imperfect waters where they can hear themselves and the long-distance communiqués they're used to trading with each other. Sound travels four times faster in water than in air; humpback sound is so loud hydrophones can pick it up from fifteen km away. Imagine how loud things have to be to drown it out! Then imagine what a relief it is to come upon Challenger, whose conical shape makes it function like a megaphone or loudspeaker, scattering your voice for miles so your loved ones can find you again.

How typical that nations drive these migrants away.

Bermuda's visitors rarely stay. Not the humpbacks, not the seabirds, not the island-archipelago's first primates, Europeans who washed up in a storm. No historical moment gave anybody any nonarbitrary, exclusive right to be Bermudian. Bermuda is no solid, bounded thing, but a flow of cultures coming and going with various tides, fluid, fragile. Which means all migrants passing through here are true Bermudians, especially those who elude each clutch and category. Migrant whales are swept up in Bermuda's tidalectics.

Tidalectics: from *tide* and *dialectic*, a portmanteau by Barbadian poet Kamau Brathwaite. Coming and going with the tide, each wave is a clash and crash of bodies, a collision of rigid land and migrant water. Their meeting is a wounding, destructive and creative one as they bleed into each other; the beach snipping bits of wave to make tide pools, the wave receding, scraping bits of beach out to the ocean. In islands' histories and cultures, moments like slave ships and snare drums come and change and recede changed; "tidalectic forces come 'from one continent/continuum, touching another, and then receding ("reading") from the island(s) into the perhaps creative chaos of the(ir) future.'"

Our refuse and weapons and entangling nets and *noise*; these things, as cruel and indelible as slavery, are the shame of our history. Brathwaite wrote:

> when men make noises
> louder than the sea's
> voices; then the rope
> will never unravel
> its knots, the branding
> iron's traveling flame that teaches
> us pain, will never be
> extinguished.

Swimming and flying in and out and through the flow are nonhuman cultures too. And the same flow of the seasons and rolling of the waves that the humpbacks ride into our shores, the same tides, yes, carry our history out to them.

❧

Mandy-Suzanne Wong's essays on sound, art, and animals appear in *Black Warrior Review, Entropy, Permafrost, Waccamaw, The Hypocrite Reader, Chaleur, Sonic Field, Breadcrumbs, Manque,* and other venues including her collection *Listen, we all bleed,* which is forthcoming from New Rivers Press.

SEISMIC TESTING

Olivia Kingery

How am I ever going to get you to listen when dolphins have to shout to each other in the ocean? We have driven them so deep, deep, deep—I don't think you've ever been that deep within yourself ever. And when I say *ever*, I mean you've never cared about the dolphins.

When you google dolphins, the first thing to come up is information on the Miami Dolphins. Scores, stats, scandals. Yet if you look just a little closer, one of the articles (which isn't the first article but, thankfully, not the last) talks about how Trump has approved seismic testing that could, would, and will harm thousands of dolphins and whales. But how can you put a number on something like that? How can you try and count how many species of animals are hiding from us under the surface of the water? The one place they should have been safe. We can't breathe underwater, so why should we be able to affect them? And yet we dig, and we dive, and we use giant air guns to find places to drill, drill, drill until we move on to the next space. Seismic tests will erase the fingerprint-calls of species who have thrived for over eleven million years, and yet we, in our newborn denial, will not listen. Because we cannot hear them over our jet engines and sonar blips; we cannot hear them over our own screaming.

These animals will push themselves towards the shore, towards what they think will be silence welcoming them, until they take their last gasp of our noise—nothing but noise. We will walk around their bodies on beaches and wonder what we can possibly do to save the lives of animals who know more than we know and still can't get away from us. We will send boats out with engines churning, churning, churning, to try and find their pods, their homes, their story—all of which we have taken and silenced and driven so far into the deep our greedy hands can't reach.

❧

Olivia Kingery is a farmer of plants and words in the Upper Peninsula of Michigan. She is an MFA candidate at Northern Michigan University where she reads for *Passages North*. When not writing, she is in the woods with her Chihuahua and Saint Bernard. She tweets @olivekingery.

SAWFISH

Tonya Wiley

Sawfish are one of the most threatened families of marine fish in the world. Their odd appearance and awesome size once made them a prized catch for recreational fishermen; their unique elongated, blade-like snouts, studded with teeth on both sides (scientifically known as a rostrum), were often kept as trophies. Though two species of sawfish were once considered abundant and common in the U.S., now only one remains, with greatly reduced numbers and geographic range. What happened to these grand fish? What caused them to vanish from much of our coastal waters? The decline can be attributed to a combination of three primary factors: over-fishing, low reproductive potential, and habitat loss.

The two species of sawfish once found in the US were the largetooth sawfish, *Pristis pristis*, and the smalltooth sawfish, *Pristis pectinata*. The largetooth sawfish was found throughout the Gulf of Mexico but was more common in the western Gulf waters of Texas and Mexico. The smalltooth sawfish ranged from Texas to North Carolina and was most plentiful in the eastern Gulf waters of Florida.

In the early 1900s, numerous postcards, photographs, and newspaper articles across the country bore scenes of fishermen hauling in sawfish to boats, docks, and beaches. Many sawfish caught recreationally were landed and displayed for photographs. Others were killed as anglers removed their saws for trophies. Commercial fishermen, finding the species a nuisance and not wanting to cut their valuable nets to remove captured fish, often killed sawfish outright rather than freeing them. Their meat was used for food, their skin for leather, their liver oil used in lamps and as a source of vitamin A. Sawfish fins became a valuable substitute for shark fin soup; their rostral teeth were used as artificial spurs in cock-fighting; their cartilage was ground up for traditional medicines; and their saws were sold as curios and ceremonial weapons.

By 1961, exploitation of the sawfish hit record heights: the last recorded catch of largetooth sawfish occurred that year in Texas, and the species has not been documented in our country's waters since. The smalltooth sawfish has fared better: though its numbers have dwindled significantly, it is still found predominately in southwest Florida, notably including Everglades National Park (ENP). The vast expanse of natural habitat within ENP, along with limited fishing pressure, likely served as a refuge for sawfish as the population was under constant pressure: they were being removed far more quickly than they were able to reproduce.

Sawfish bear live young, take many years to reach sexual maturity, and produce very few offspring per reproductive cycle. Born at about two feet in length, juvenile sawfish rely on very shallow coastal and estuarine waters for ample food and safety from predators, such as sharks, during the first years of their life. However, these shallow coastal waters are the same areas that have been converted to waterfront development. Much of the natural shoreline vegetation has been developed into seawalls, beaches, marinas, roads, canals, and docks.

Therefore, the natural vegetation and shallow habitats previously used by sawfish as important protective nursery areas have been greatly reduced in quantity and all but eliminated in some areas.

With severe threats to their mortality and habitat, and unable to reproduce their numbers quickly enough to combat the danger, the US population of smalltooth sawfish hit critical lows. Due to the dramatic decline, the smalltooth sawfish was classified as endangered in 2003, making it the first fully marine fish and first elasmobranch (sharks, skates, and rays) protected by the Endangered Species Act. The largetooth sawfish joined the list in 2011, though they are believed to be locally extinct, unlikely to return to US waters.

To preserve smalltooth sawfish numbers, many institutions conduct various research activities on the biology, behavior, and ecology of endangered smalltooth sawfish in the United States. These partners include state and federal government institutions, universities, nonprofits, NGOs, and international organizations. The results of these research projects are used to inform management decisions and enhance recovery efforts for this endangered species.

Collecting Sawfish Data

Researchers collect information about sawfish using a variety of methodologies: (1) sawfish captured during research field surveys for the species, (2) sawfish incidentally caught in federal fisheries, (3) sawfish carcasses, and (4) tissue samples collected from antique sawfish rostra (saws).

Research field surveys for smalltooth sawfish are the most important method for collecting data. A variety of survey methods are used to capture live sawfish for scientific purposes, including longline, rod-and-reel, and gillnets. Once captured, measurements and samples are taken from each sawfish prior to tagging and release. These surveys are instrumental in monitoring trends in the abundance of the population.

Fishery observers aboard commercial fishing vessels are trained to measure, sample, and tag any sawfish incidentally captured in federally-permitted fisheries. These chance opportunities provide valuable insight into the locations where fisheries overlap with sawfish and the condition of sawfish upon release.

Necropsies of sawfish that have died in the wild provide the opportunity to collect data necessary for understanding age, growth, maturity, and reproduction. Carcass recoveries provide valuable opportunities because these data are especially important and can only be collected through dissection, as researchers are currently not comfortable sacrificing any healthy individuals of this critically endangered species.

Before sawfish were listed as Endangered in 2003, sawfish rostra were considered unique "trophies," and many have been retained in both public and private collections. To find sawfish rostra, which can provide valuable DNA data, researchers scour online databases, ask the public about sawfish rostra they own or have seen, and contact curators at museums, educational centers, aquariums, universities, and other public institutions. The removal or sale of rostra is now illegal in the United States.

Samples

Small tissue samples are collected during field capture of live sawfish, and from old rostra, for genetic and stable isotope studies. Genetics are useful in understanding population structure, diversity within the population, and both the size and health of the current population in comparison to the historical one. Scientists are also using genetics to determine whether there are significant movement and genetic exchange between the US and Bahamas populations of smalltooth sawfish. Stable isotopic analyses are run on tissue samples and compared to a variety of potential prey items in the environment to determine the diet and trophic position of smalltooth sawfish within the food web.

Blood samples are collected from sawfish to investigate reproductive status and stress physiology. Hormones within the blood are used to assess reproductive maturity and timing. Blood samples for stress physiology are used to assess post-release mortality risk from a variety of fisheries and gears.

Acoustic Tracking

Scientists are using state-of-the-art technology to track the movements of smalltooth sawfish. This tracking involves capturing the animals, equipping them with acoustic transmitters, and releasing them. Depending on the objectives of the project, scientists may track them from a boat using hydrophones to determine short-term microhabitat use or set up a network of in-water receivers (acoustic listening stations) to track longer-term, broad-scale movements. Acoustic transmitters can be active for up to ten years.

Satellite Tagging

Larger juvenile and adult sawfish caught during surveys are also sometimes fitted with GPS satellite tags. Because far less is known about these larger animals, researchers hope that satellite tags can reveal important adult habitats, movements, and migrations. Satellite tagging studies to date have shown that larger sawfish spend a large portion of their time in shallow coastal waters, with periodic excursions to deeper waters off the shelf edge.

Handling and Release Guidelines

While it is technically illegal to catch a sawfish (except with a research permit or in a fishery where incidental take has been authorized), captures do occur while fishing for other species. Any sawfish caught while fishing must be released as quickly as possible. The guidelines below were developed to aid anglers in quickly and safely releasing incidentally caught sawfish.

The number one rule to remember when handling and releasing a sawfish is to always leave it in the water. Do not lift it out of the water onto your boat or a pier, and do not drag it onshore. Because of the ESA protections, it is illegal to possess a sawfish; therefore, removing it from the water is a clear violation of the law. This also ensures the safety of both the sawfish and the angler. Sawfish are powerful animals that can whip their saw very quickly, which can cause serious injury to the angler and the sawfish.

Sawfish are extremely susceptible to entanglement in recreational fishing lines and commercial nets. Mishandling and the purposeful injury or killing of captured sawfish is both illegal and detrimental to the recovery of the population. Never use a gaff on a sawfish you have caught, and never remove the rostrum. Sawfish use their rostrum for detecting and catching food, so, in addition to being illegal, removal of the rostrum severely limits the animal's chance to find enough food to survive.

General Release Guidelines:
- Leave the sawfish in the water—never lift or drag it onto a boat, pier, or shore
- Never remove the saw (rostrum) or injure the animal in any way
- Use extreme caution when handling and releasing sawfish as the saw can thrash violently from side to side
- Never use a gaff or rope to secure a sawfish

If hooked:
- Leave the sawfish, especially the gills, in the water
- If it can be done safely, untangle any line wrapped around the saw
- Cut the line as close to the hook as possible

If tangled in a cast net:
- Leave the sawfish, especially the gills, in the water
- Untangle and cut the net, removing as much of it as possible from the animal
- Release the sawfish quickly

Population Monitoring Through Encounter Reports

One of the best methods of monitoring the population as it recovers is the use of public sawfish encounters. If you catch or see a sawfish, take a quick photograph of it, estimate its size, note your location, and share the information with scientists. The details of your sightings or catches help to monitor the population and track recovery progress. You can share your information by calling 1-844-4-SAWFISH (1-844-472-9347) or visiting www.SawfishRecovery.org. Information about historic catches or the location of any old sawfish rostra is also greatly appreciated.

International Sawfish Day

Sawfishes are among the world's most threatened elasmobranchs and yet few people know about these amazingly unique animals. There are five species of sawfish in the world and all are classified as critically endangered or endangered by The International Union for Conservation of Nature (IUCN).

Founded by the European and American Associations of Zoos and Aquariums and the Sawfish Conservation Society,

International Sawfish Day is an annual event held on October 17 each year to raise awareness of these vulnerable rays and to highlight the threats they face in order to safeguard their future. Organizations around the world, including aquariums, museums, zoos, schools, conservation agencies, research facilities, and other institutions and organizations, hold celebrations and events, share messages and images on social media, help spread the word about endangered sawfish, and raise funds to support sawfish research programs.

The ultimate goal of the Endangered Species Act is to conserve listed species to the point they are recovered and no longer need the protections afforded by the Act. Will sawfish in the United States recover? The smalltooth sawfish just might make a comeback; the population is already showing promising signs following these extensive protective measures. Continued proper management and protections of the species and its habitats will ensure that sawfish numbers increase, and that their range expands.

Tonya Wiley grew up far from saltwater in Michigan and north Texas, but developed a love for the ocean during family vacations to Florida, and caught her first shark while fishing with her dad in Charlotte Harbor. Following a stint in the US Navy, she received a Bachelor of Science degree in Marine Fisheries from Texas A&M University at Galveston.

Tonya is an authority on the biology and ecology of smalltooth sawfish, having engaged in nearly two decades of groundbreaking field research on the species. She also excels at sawfish outreach and education, and was recently appointed to lead the NOAA's Smalltooth Sawfish Recovery Implementation Team, after many years of service as an appointed member. Ms. Wiley produces monthly issues of "Sawfish News" to highlight timely information on sawfish research and conservation. She has developed and led workshops to train researchers and the public on proper handling, release, data recording, and reporting procedures for incidentally caught sawfish. Ms. Wiley regularly gives sawfish presentations at professional and public events, and has co-authored several peer-reviewed publications on sawfish. Tonya currently serves as Secretary for the American Elasmobranch Society, is a board member and Secretary of the Sawfish Conservation Society, and is the Treasurer and Chair of the curriculum committee for Coastal Brigade-Texas Brigades. Tonya is the founder and president of Havenworth Coastal Conservation, a project of The Ocean Foundation dedicated to promoting the sustainable use and conservation of marine resources through research, outreach, and education.

Tonya lives with her husband, Chris, on Terra Ceia Bay in Florida, and enjoys any activity that gets her on the water, including fishing, boating, snorkeling, kayaking, and paddle boarding. Her favorite place to fish is in Everglades National Park, particularly Ponce de Leon Bay.

Tonya Wiley, President
Havenworth Coastal Conservation
5120 Beacon Road
Palmetto, Florida, USA 34221
tonya@havenworth.org

SOME SWIM

Lorraine Jeffery

away, some propulse, some try
to crawl, some too
slow or stuck
litter ocean floor. Suffocated

crabs in low-oxygen
hypoxia water. Dead rock
fish on sandy shoals. Oregon
coast of my childhood, clam chowder
warmth, bustling

processing plants,
a cousin's red
and white fishing boat. Scientists
find dead zones from Florence
to Newport. Warming

ocean holds less water while winds
and currents change. With buoys
and ocean-roaming gliders
they study, but don't

resolve a damn thing. A new
normal? Waves crash
black lava above a still
ocean floor.

෭

Lorraine Jeffery earned her bachelor's degree in English and her MLIS in library science. She has won poetry prizes in state and national contests and has published over sixty poems in various publications, including *Clockhouse*, *Kindred*, *Calliope*, *Ibbetson Street*, and *Rockhurst Review*. She has also published short stories and essays.

WITHOUT MAKING A -CENE: ON IMMORTALITY AND WARMING SEAS

Liberty Lawson

alchemy

*The transmutation of matter; turning sun into stone, like a coral.
Turning oceans into plastic, like a human.*

The Great Barrier Reef is a paradox and a miracle. From above, azure ribbons snake along thousands of kilometres of coastline, punctuated by ellipses of calcium carbonate cathedrals. These structures are visible from space, and yet the animals that thrust them from the deep are too small to be seen by human eyes. Corals are the Earth's greatest architects, fragile conglomerations of animal, flower, and mineral. They work on vastly different scales than us, flourishing over eons rather than seasons: reefs recede and reincarnate as seas rise and fall, freeze and thaw. But, in our current human-dominated geological age, the Anthropocene, corals bleach white overnight in billowing swathes. Jellyfish bloom in murky harbor depths. Out on the wide horizon, cuttlefish dance in the lights of cargo ships, turtles catch plastic bags, and whales wander alone in waters too wide to ever meet. Our world is spiralling too quickly to catch up.

abhinivesa

The root of all the poisons of the human mind, according to the ancient sage Patanjali. Manifesting as a fear of illness, hunger, falling, fire, and, ultimately, death.

71

In January 2019, the death of Masazo Nonaka in Ashoror, Hokkaido made headlines worldwide. Nonaka died peacefully, in his sleep, during the early hours of the morning. Born on July 25, 1905, he was the oldest man in the world. In the one hundred thirteen years since his birth, humans have invented plastic, synthetic ammonia, vaccinations, GMO crops that override the seasons, planes that transcend continents, spaceships that overcome gravity. We have mastered agriculture, medicine, and industry to transcend the limits of our existence. Our population has swelled from one billion at the dawn of the century to the current 7.7 billion. Our life expectancy has skyrocketed, yet death has never been closer. We can remain cognitively removed from its reality; we now have hospices and crematoriums, glass windows and pre-packaged meat—but in our frantic efforts to ensure our generation's survival, to further ourselves from our own endings, we have created an excess of carbon and plastic that is now suffocating us and the planet. The Anthropocene marks the sixth global extinction—and the first for which one species alone is responsible.

hyperobject

Multidimensional objects that extend through space and time, too vast and complex to be imagined, reduced, localised, categorised, cleaned up.

Even at the dawn of the twenty-first century, coral reefs were the still wonders of the world. The greenhouse effect was talked about in abstract, distant terms. A problem for our children's children. A problem for generations we would never meet. The biggest threat to coral was the crown-of-thorns starfish. The threats of the Anthropocene, however, are problems of scale; they are generational, global problems, hyperobjects that transcend individual human experience and observation. Problems that cannot be cleaned up. You can point to a starfish, but you can't point to carbon dioxide or the swirling gyres of ocean microplastics. Corals also exist beyond the convenience and linearity of human space and time. They are complex symbiotic organisms with little regard for neat boundaries and taxonomic categories. Corals, as we think of them, are microcosmic colonies of millions of tiny animals called polyps. Like us, they cannot help but transform their landscapes. The polyps excrete calcium carbonate, a mineral which builds up to form the solid limestone substrate of the reef. The individual polyps are each just a few millimetres wide, only a mouth and a few tentacles. Their tissues are home to photosynthetic zooxanthellae, an even more minuscule organism with the somewhat miraculous job of turning sunlight into energy so the polyp can build its limestone palace.

For millennia, that has been enough. But in 2016, the Great Barrier Reef, which covers 350,000 square kilometres along the north-east coast of Australia, underwent a massive coral bleaching, the worst in recorded history. High temperatures and little cloud cover resulted in record-breaking sea-surface temperatures. Headlines called it "a once-in-a-lifetime event"—until the following summer, when it happened again. A long and blistering El Niño hindered the cooling monsoon, and the corals that survived the 2016 bleaching were once again engulfed by relentlessly fiery tides. When waters are too warm, the brightly coloured zooxanthellae slow down the production of energy, and the polyp spits them out. Real estate on the reef is usually lucrative, and the coral expects new tenants to swiftly repopulate it and colour its flesh once more. But if the water remains hot, the coral begins to starve. Brown algae spreads across the surface, and the skeleton begins eroding back into sand. More than half the corals died.

-cene

Suffix; denoting a recent geological period; a vast amount of time. Derived from the Greek word kainos, meaning new.

There have been five mass extinctions in our planet's history so far. There have been rising seas and ice ages and climate changes. However, these have all taken hundreds of thousands, if not millions, of years to transform the planet. The Anthropocene, defined by its swiftness, is an infinitesimal blink of the geological eye, so swift that we don't yet have words for it. We can pace out the distance from a paper Sun to Jupiter by counting steps in the schoolyard, but we can't imagine the complexity and chaos we have created in the past decades. We humans only have words for tiny things. We know of plastic straws, but not the toxic bacterial colonies evolving on microplastics in the ocean. Our thermometers measure summer afternoons, not decade-long droughts that lead to uncontrollable wildfires. We fill our car with gas, and we forget about the eighty billion other tanks that are filled each year. We trace a dotted line onto a map—a marine reserve to protect a fragment of ocean—as though climate change cares about cartography. We only know the tiny things. The polyps, not the reefs.

smack

Collective noun; jellyfish.

As the first pallid swathes unfurled across the coral reefs, another animal was revelling in the warming tides. Jellyfish are a close cousin of corals, both tentacular cnidaria. Millions of years ago, when corals attached to rock to begin their tessellated lives of sessile but symbiotic alchemy, the soft and lone-wandering jellyfish ventured out into the tides in search of prey. The lack of complex physical features makes jellyfish extremely adaptable to a range of climates. They don't rely solely on temperature-sensitive photosynthesis. They can survive freezing depths and turbid, polluted harbours. They can survive through time, too. In 1996, a tiny species of jelly, the *Turritopsis dohrnii*, floating off the coast of Japan, was discovered to be immortal. The jellyfish cycles and re-cycles through its life stages, beyond possibility, beyond death, back into youth.

Their soft transparency leaves little in the way of atolls or skyscrapers, but jellyfish don't need fossilised legacies. They are not as preoccupied with being remembered as we are. They are unlike the eucalypt forests that are engulfed by wildfires so that the earth is clear for next year's saplings to unfurl. Unlike the corals that hibernate, reincarnate, and patiently terraform their palaces over millennia. Unlike humans, who tried as best they could to build a world for their children to survive. The *Turritopsis* floats in the ocean all alone, unconcerned with past and future.

smack

Onomatopoeic; the sound of glass bottles packed with potassium nitrate exploding under coral reefs.

For decades, we dropped dynamite onto coral reefs. The shockwave killed the fish in the area and sent them floating to the surface. Reefs were decimated, and coral skeletons were then hauled to shore and used as building materials. Their skyscrapers line our horizons. But, of course, corals have a geomorphological function: they act as a breakwall that protects the shore from erosion, wave damage, and flooding. The more we take from the reefs, the higher the seas will rise. The skyscrapers will sink back into the depths, back to where those tiny zooxanthellae first created stone from sun. Such is the cyclical nature of this world. When humans leave this planet, the tides will change, and the dark slime of algae will recede back to the depths. In the one hundred thirteen years since Mr. Nonaka was born, the average coral would have grown less than a hundred centimetres, but many of the biggest porites boulders could be thousands of years old. Young, compared to the rocks beneath them. They have seen ashen skies, frozen seas, wars—they have worn scars and healed. It won't be on our time, but life will return to the incarnadine waters left by the Anthropocene. It always does.

References

Gerardo Ceballos, Paul R. Ehrlich, and Rodolfo Dirzo. 2017. "Biological annihilation via the ongoing sixth mass extinction signaled by vertebrate population losses and declines." *PNAS*. 114 (30) 6089-6096.

Terry Hughes and James Kerry. 2017. "Back-to-back bleaching has now hit two-thirds of the Great Barrier Reef". *The Conversation*. URL: https://theconversation.com/back-to-back-bleaching-has-now-hit-two-thirds-of-the-great-barrier-reef-76092

Timothy Morton. 2013. *Hyperobjects: Philosophy and Ecology after the End of the World*. Minneapolis: University of Minnesota Press.

Stefano Piraino, Ferdinando Boero, Brigitte Aeschbach and Volker Schmid. 1996. "Reversing the Life Cycle: Medusae Transforming into Polyps and Cell Transdifferentiation in Turritopsis nutricula (Cnidaria, Hydrozoa)." *Biological Bulletin.* 190 (3) 302-312.

Sri Swami Satchidananda, 2012. "The Yoga Sutras of Patanjali." *Integral Yoga Publications*, Virginia.

ॐ

Liberty Lawson is a writer, a researcher at the Sydney Environment Institute, a Blue Charter Research Fellow with the ACU, and an interdisciplinary PhD student at the University of Sydney. She has a background in marine biology, coral ecology, and philosophy, and, as an academic, she works with artificial coral reefs, conservation policy, and science communication.

As a writer, she is fascinated by micro- and macro-spatiotemporal scales, hybrid ecologies, and what our human understanding of these spaces reveals about us as a species.

THE WATERS

Jayne Marek

is a poem about garbage garbage
or will this abstract, hollow junk seem beautiful
and necessary...
—A. R. Ammons, "Garbage"

you lived under the lake effect and I live
under the arms of the Pacific

Ocean effect that pushes up with every tide
the detritus of what used to be living

along unstable shores and surfaces that, like most
of the earth's places, do not care for human

imposition: fishing and boating and tidepooling
and shipping and cruising all occur in hopes

of avoiding the notice especially of confused
seas, as the Pacific Ocean effect means knowing

how tenuously one trims the thinnest
borders of this profound medium

that mediates between wind currents
and the guiding processes of the bowls

and basins of rock in hundreds of formations
that ultimately balance the unthinkable

tonnage of ocean water, in what has to be
delicate and ponderous suspension over

the steaming fissures of the Mariana Trench,
where there are monsters unimaginable

to humans, who are used to
the recognizable monstrosity of

each other: sea monsters of course
being a misnomer since these filamentous

amorphous mollusks or leatherskinned fishes
or what-have-you are perfectly developed for

living in the hot flow from hydrothermal vents
boiling with the deepest chemical reactions on earth

that, even so, cannot melt minute pieces of trash
tracing undersea streams (so many levels

of movement to bring down the plastic bags
and microbeads that were meant to clean

rich people's faces and now linger
in oily fingerprints floating throughout

the water column) and, in the decades
since you pointed out to us our obvious

idiocy, we have continued with the same
mania to discard our productions along

with our ability to breathe and eat and drink,
while we make make and make, making us

what we cannot sustain: and yet here
we are leaving fragments of polymers,

polyethylene, polypropylene, polyvinyl,
polystyrene, words we have taken into

our minds and bodies so deeply that,
since we are so much composed of water,

especially in our lungs and brains,
we with our cancers, unbeautiful, unfortunate,

do indeed resemble the Pacific Ocean
garbage patch, inside and out

AT THIS SHORE

Jayne Marek

All will die from water
 its overzealous love
  or its selfish paucity

I run the sea rim dodging
 turn of tide
  fingers of wrack

as world remakes
 shores into stones into sand
  bodies into ribbons

A beached sculpin
 gasps its ocean life
  and onshore death

Its eyes face forward
 like mine
  toward mine as if

the opaque lens
 of its extirpation
  sees that somehow

its death in eelgrass
　shallows is my fault
　　as if I could change it

Perhaps there is mercy
　in quick death
　　not knowing

the other creatures who
　also will die
　　on a fool's errand

ॐ

Jayne Marek's poems and photographs appear in *One, Light, Grub Street, The Cortland Review, Slipstream, The Lake, Stonecoast Review, Spillway, Women's Studies Quarterly, Sin Fronteras, Notre Dame Review,* and elsewhere. She provided color cover art for *Silk Road, Bombay Gin, Amsterdam Quarterly's 2018 Yearbook,* and *The Bend,* as well as for her books of poetry *In and Out of Rough Water* (2017) and *The Tree Surgeon Dreams of Bowling* (2018). Twice nominated for a Pushcart Prize, she was a finalist for the *Up North* poetry prize, the *Naugatuck River Review* poetry contest, the David Martinson–Meadowhawk Prize, the Ex Ophidia Poetry Book Prize, and the Ryan R. Gibbs photography award.

What is there to do?

Emma C. Bush

The ocean is dying,
this much is true.
The ocean is crying—
what is there to do?

Its beaches are plastic,
its corals are white,
its waters are filthy,
and fish a rare sight.

All of the creatures
who live underneath
are facing disaster,
from the waves to the reef.

The ocean is dying,
but what can I do?
For all of my life
it's been up to you—

Yes, it's been up to you,
to the people in power
who won't listen to me
from way up in their tower.

You won't listen to me;
You're too young, you say,
but I see what you don't
on each shore and each bay.

I see the sea dying
and I know what I'll do—
I'll keep speaking up
'til you see what is true:

That the ocean needs help
as soon as can be,
and we all have to change
or we may lose the sea.

We may lose the sea,
all its beauty and magic,
from fishes to whales
and all that's pelagic.

So I will not stop trying,
until something is done,
until somebody listens
to a kid's opinion.

The ocean is dying—
this much is true.
The ocean is crying,
but I know what I'll do.

෴

Emma is a seventeen-year-old scuba diver and aspiring marine biologist from Blacksburg, Virginia who loves the ocean more than anything else in the universe. She has always been fascinated with anything and everything marine, and feels very strongly about conservation issues. She hopes to spread awareness about the issues facing our oceans, and do everything she can to help solve them, from raising awareness through art and writing, to educating those in her community, to conducting research.

She was inspired to submit to this anthology because she believes that awareness is a major step in solving any issue, and that a range of diverse perspectives, including a range of ages, is the most effective way of raising awareness.